GRAPHIC DINOSAURS

ELASMOSAURUS

THE LONG-NECKED SWIMMER

ILLUSTRATED BY TERRY RILEY

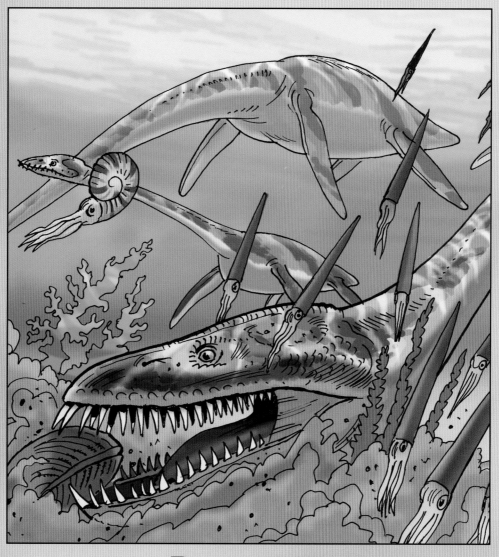

PowerKiDS press

New York

Published in 2009 by The Rosen Publishing Group, Inc
29 East 21st Street, New York, NY 10010

Designed and produced by
David West Books

Designed and written by Gary Jeffrey
Editor: Ronne Randall
Consultant: Steve Parker, Senior Scientific Fellow, Zoological Society of London
Photographic credits: 5t, Ballista (http://en.wikipedia.org); 5bl, Peter Cheyne; 5br, Dennis Otten; 31,
Mike Everhart.

Library of Congress Cataloging-in-Publication Data

Jeffrey, Gary
Elasmosaurus : the long-necked swimmer / Gary Jeffrey.
p. cm. — (Graphic dinosaurs)
Includes index.
ISBN 978-1-4358-2505-5 (library binding)
ISBN 978-1-4042-7715-1 (pbk.)
ISBN 978-1-4042-7719-9 (6 pack)
1. Elasmosaurus—Juvenile literature. I. Title.
QE862.P4J44 2009
567.9'37—dc22

2008003881

Manufactured in China

CONTENTS

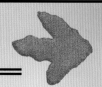

WHAT IS AN ELASMOSAURUS?

ELASMOSAURUS MEANS "THIN PLATE LIZARD"

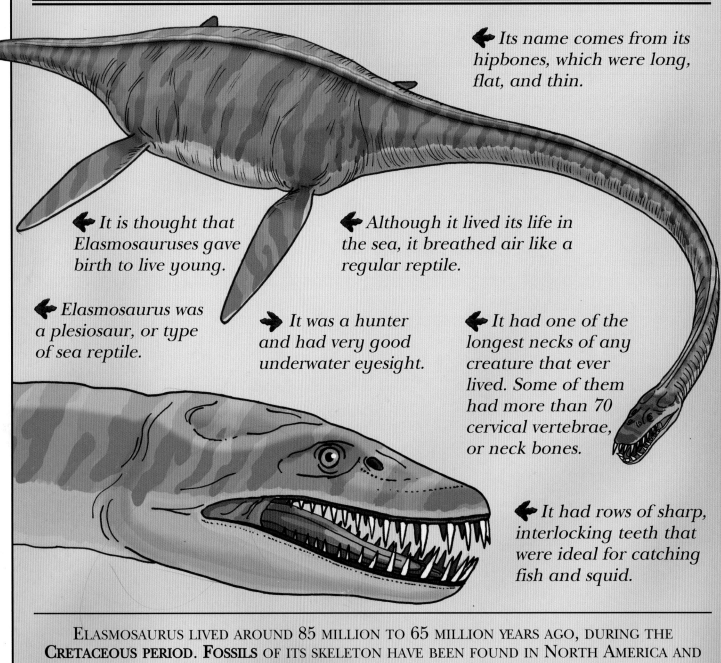

← *Its name comes from its hipbones, which were long, flat, and thin.*

← *It is thought that Elasmosauruses gave birth to live young.*

← *Although it lived its life in the sea, it breathed air like a regular reptile.*

← *Elasmosaurus was a plesiosaur, or type of sea reptile.*

→ *It was a hunter and had very good underwater eyesight.*

← *It had one of the longest necks of any creature that ever lived. Some of them had more than 70 cervical vertebrae, or neck bones.*

← *It had rows of sharp, interlocking teeth that were ideal for catching fish and squid.*

ELASMOSAURUS LIVED AROUND 85 MILLION TO 65 MILLION YEARS AGO, DURING THE CRETACEOUS PERIOD. FOSSILS OF ITS SKELETON HAVE BEEN FOUND IN NORTH AMERICA AND OTHER PARTS OF THE WORLD.

← Adult Elasmosauruses measured up to 45 feet (14 m) long. Half of this length was their necks. They weighed about 2.2 tons (1,995 kg).

PLESIOSAURS

"A snake strung through a turtle" was how someone once described a long-necked plesiosaur. Elasmosaurus lived in the large, shallow ocean that covered modern-day Kansas. It was the last long-necked plesiosaur to become **extinct**. Elasmosaurus is unlike any modern-day animal.

A fossilized plesiosaur's flipper.

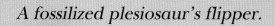

FLIPPERS FOR FEET

We know by looking at their flipper bones that plesiosaurs originally came from four-legged animals. Plesiosaur fossils clearly show finger, wrist, and arm bones.

MOVEMENT

It was originally thought that Elasmosauruses rowed their flippers back and forth like the oars on a boat. We now think they "flapped" them up and down in a similar way to penguins and sea lions. This would have made them slow, graceful swimmers.

LIFESTYLE

Elasmosauruses probably lived like dolphins. Dolphins have sharp teeth to catch fish and squid. Elasmosauruses may even have traveled in **pods**, like dolphins do.

PART ONE... THE NEW ARRIVALS

IT IS 70 MILLION YEARS AGO. THREE NEWBORN ELASMOSAURUSES ARE SWIMMING IN THE COOL WATERS OF THE WESTERN INTERIOR SEAWAY IN WHAT IS NOW KANSAS.

THE POD HAS COME TO THIS QUIET STRETCH OF WATER TO AVOID THE OTHER PREDATORS, BUT THEY ARE NOT ALONE.

A PAIR OF CLIDASTESES, SMALL SEA REPTILES, HAVE BEEN STUDYING THEM CAREFULLY.

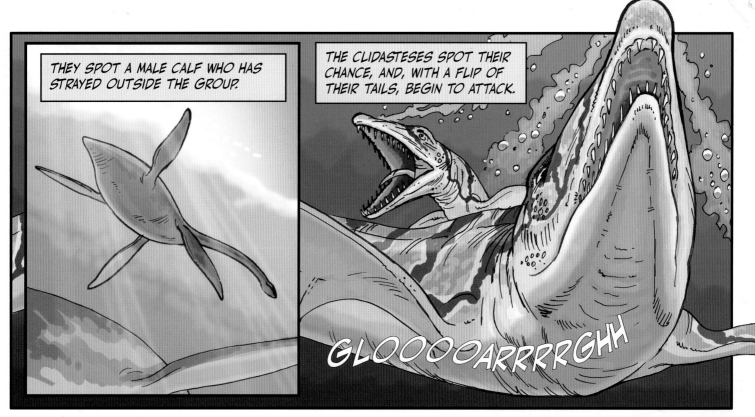

THEY SPOT A MALE CALF WHO HAS STRAYED OUTSIDE THE GROUP.

THE CLIDASTESES SPOT THEIR CHANCE, AND, WITH A FLIP OF THEIR TAILS, BEGIN TO ATTACK.

GLOOOOARRRRGHH

THE CLIDASTESES ARE FAST, BUT AN OLDER ELASMOSAURUS HAS SPOTTED THE DANGER TO THE CALF.

GLOOOBLAAAGHH

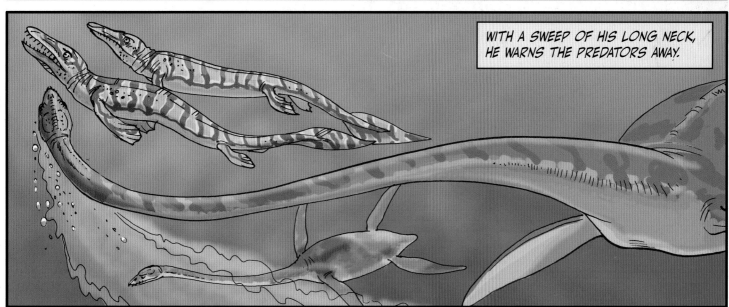

WITH A SWEEP OF HIS LONG NECK, HE WARNS THE PREDATORS AWAY.

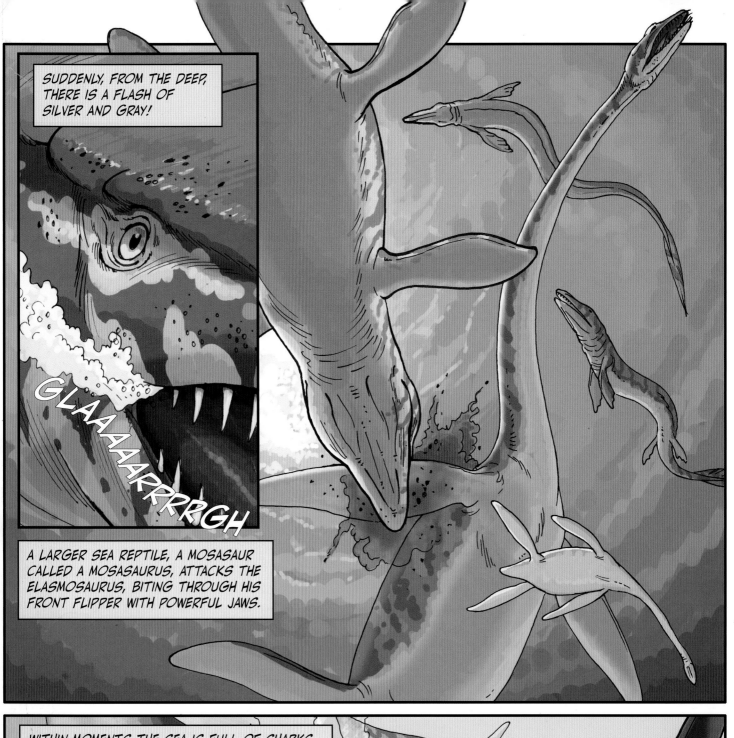

SUDDENLY, FROM THE DEEP, THERE IS A FLASH OF SILVER AND GRAY!

GLAAAARRRRGH

A LARGER SEA REPTILE, A MOSASAUR CALLED A MOSASAURUS, ATTACKS THE ELASMOSAURUS, BITING THROUGH HIS FRONT FLIPPER WITH POWERFUL JAWS.

WITHIN MOMENTS THE SEA IS FULL OF SHARKS SPEEDING IN TOWARD THE SMELL OF BLOOD.

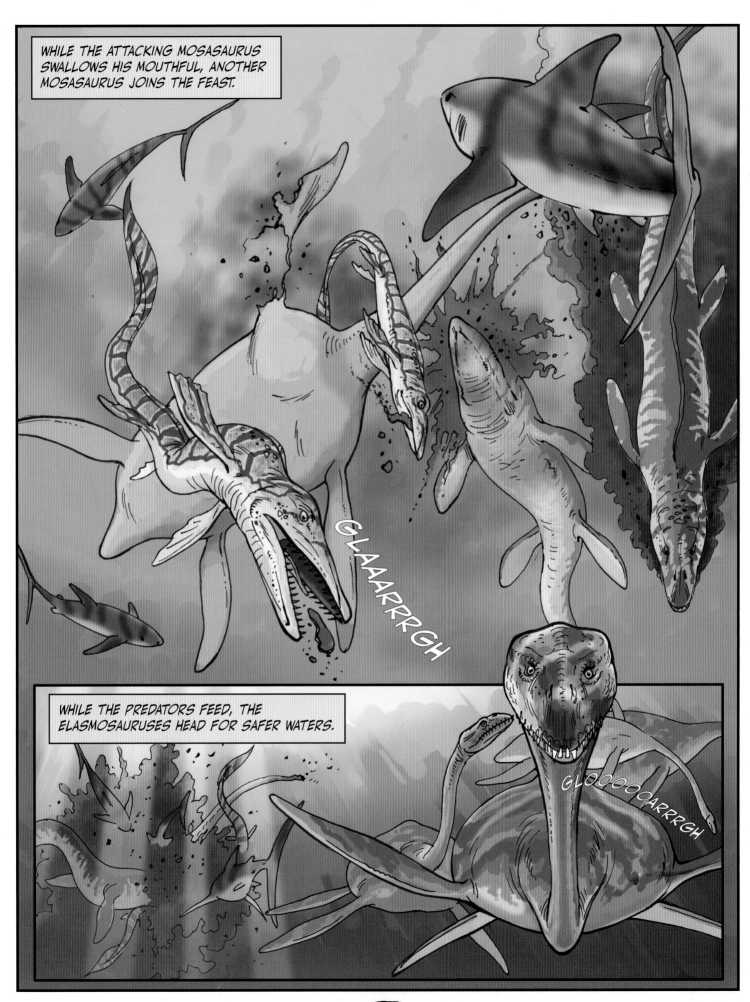

WHILE THE ATTACKING MOSASAURUS SWALLOWS HIS MOUTHFUL, ANOTHER MOSASAURUS JOINS THE FEAST.

GLAAARRRGH

WHILE THE PREDATORS FEED, THE ELASMOSAURUSES HEAD FOR SAFER WATERS.

GLOOOOOARRRGH

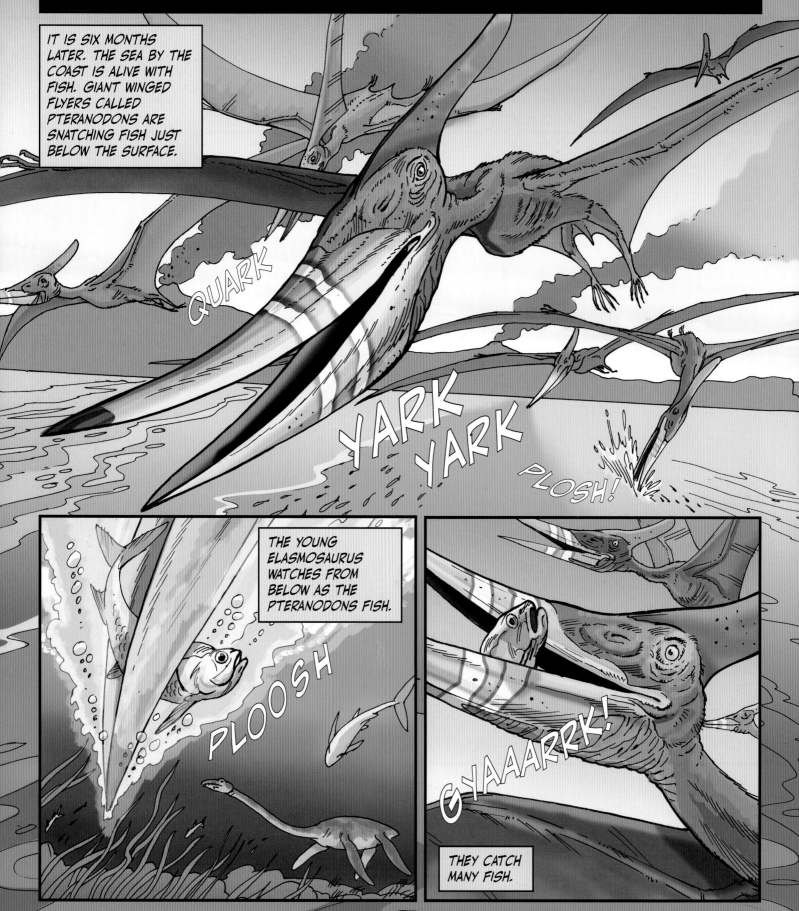

THE ELASMOSAURUS LOOKS AT THE FISH.

HE FEELS HUNGRY. BUT HOW TO CATCH ONE?

MOVING HIS FLIPPERS, HE **DARTS** TOWARD THE SCHOOL, BUT THE FISH ARE TOO QUICK.

HE CHASES A FISH.

THE FISH IS A FAST SWIMMER, BUT THE ELASMOSAURUS IS CLOSING IN.

HE IS ABOUT TO BITE WHEN THERE IS AN EXPLOSION OF BUBBLES. THE FISH HAS **VANISHED!**

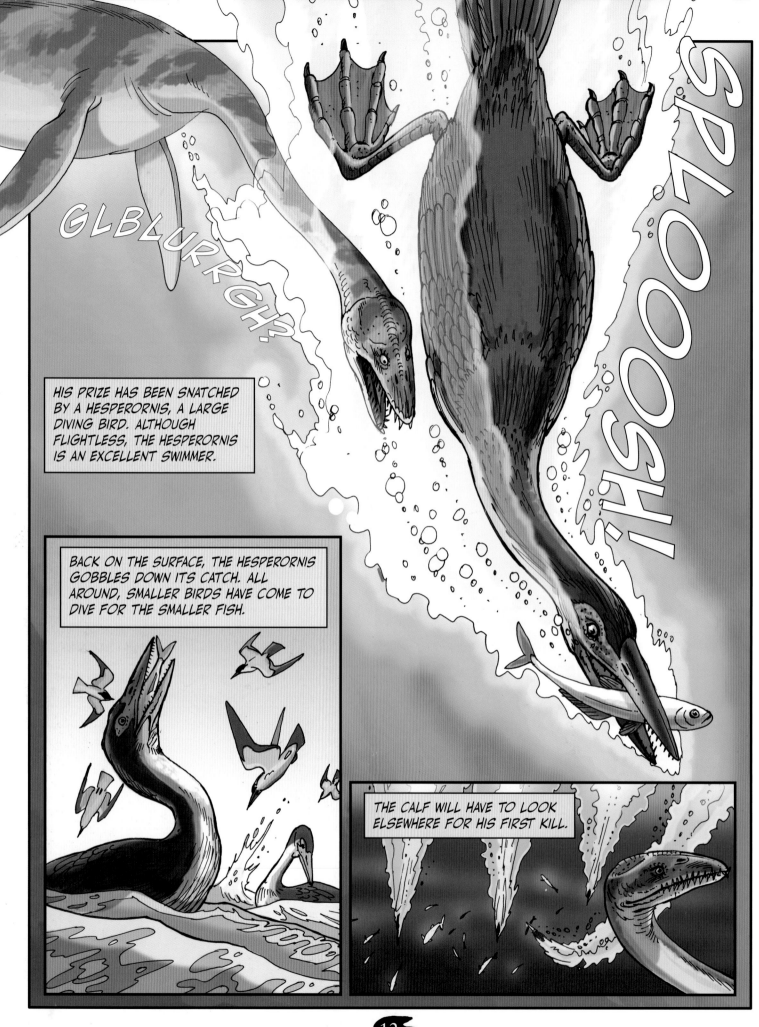

GLBLURRGH?

SPLOOOSH!

HIS PRIZE HAS BEEN SNATCHED BY A HESPERORNIS, A LARGE DIVING BIRD. ALTHOUGH FLIGHTLESS, THE HESPERORNIS IS AN EXCELLENT SWIMMER.

BACK ON THE SURFACE, THE HESPERORNIS GOBBLES DOWN ITS CATCH. ALL AROUND, SMALLER BIRDS HAVE COME TO DIVE FOR THE SMALLER FISH.

THE CALF WILL HAVE TO LOOK ELSEWHERE FOR HIS FIRST KILL.

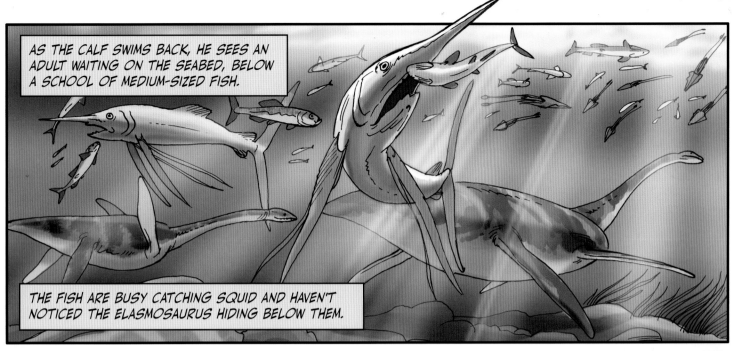

AS THE CALF SWIMS BACK, HE SEES AN ADULT WAITING ON THE SEABED, BELOW A SCHOOL OF MEDIUM-SIZED FISH.

THE FISH ARE BUSY CATCHING SQUID AND HAVEN'T NOTICED THE ELASMOSAURUS HIDING BELOW THEM.

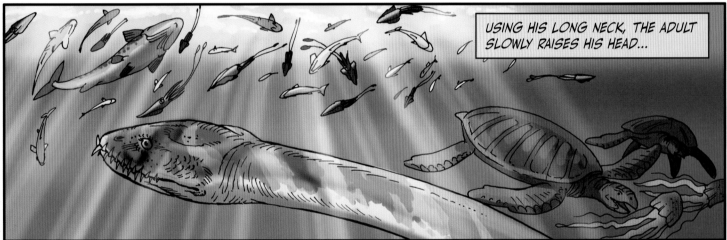

USING HIS LONG NECK, THE ADULT SLOWLY RAISES HIS HEAD...

...RIGHT UNDER THE FEEDING FISH. THEN...

...HE STRIKES!

SPLOOOSH!!

HAVING SEEN THE LESSON, THE YOUNG ELASMOSAURUS CAREFULLY SWIMS UNDER A SQUID...

...AND GETS HIS FIRST CATCH.

GKARRRGH

HE HAS JUST SWALLOWED IT WHEN HE IS HURRIED AWAY. SOME UNWELCOME VISITORS ARE ARRIVING.

SWOOOOSH

THEY ARE MOSASAURS CALLED PLATECARPUSES, SQUID FEEDERS WHO TRAVEL IN GROUPS. THEIR APPEARANCE FRIGHTENS THE ELASMOSAURUSES AWAY.

GLAAAAARGH

GLAUMPH

14

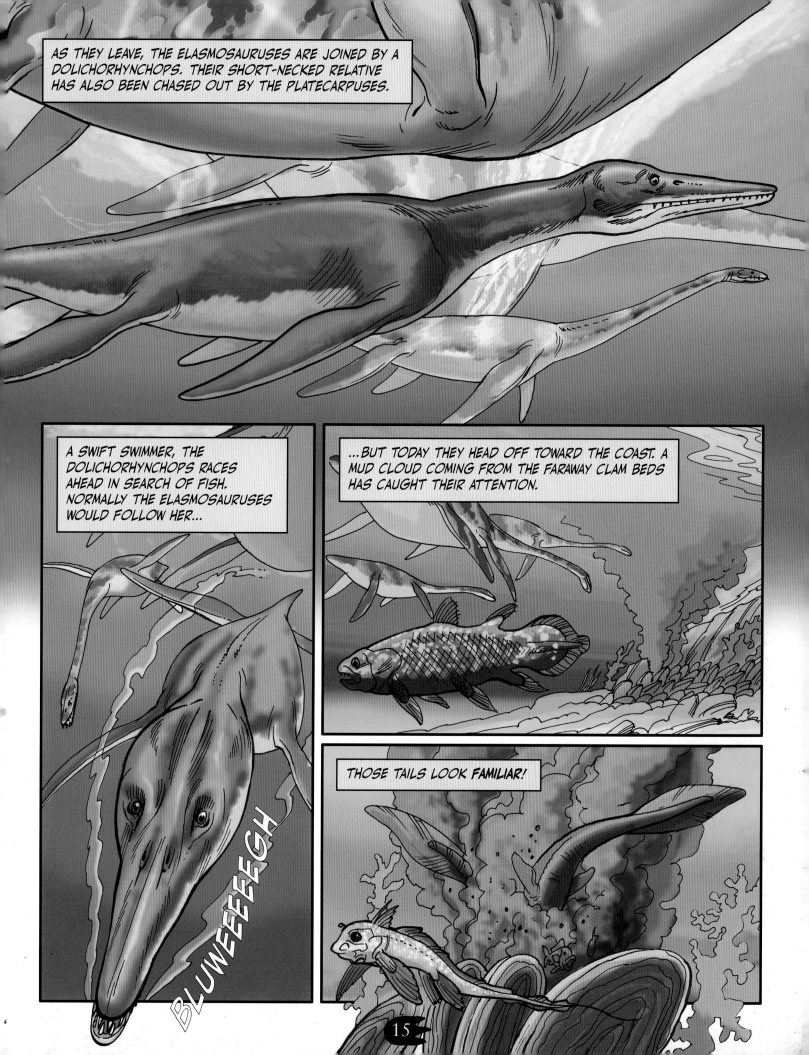

AS THEY LEAVE, THE ELASMOSAURUSES ARE JOINED BY A DOLICHORHYNCHOPS. THEIR SHORT-NECKED RELATIVE HAS ALSO BEEN CHASED OUT BY THE PLATECARPUSES.

A SWIFT SWIMMER, THE DOLICHORHYNCHOPS RACES AHEAD IN SEARCH OF FISH. NORMALLY THE ELASMOSAURUSES WOULD FOLLOW HER...

...BUT TODAY THEY HEAD OFF TOWARD THE COAST. A MUD CLOUD COMING FROM THE FARAWAY CLAM BEDS HAS CAUGHT THEIR ATTENTION.

THOSE TAILS LOOK FAMILIAR!

BLUWEEEEGH

15

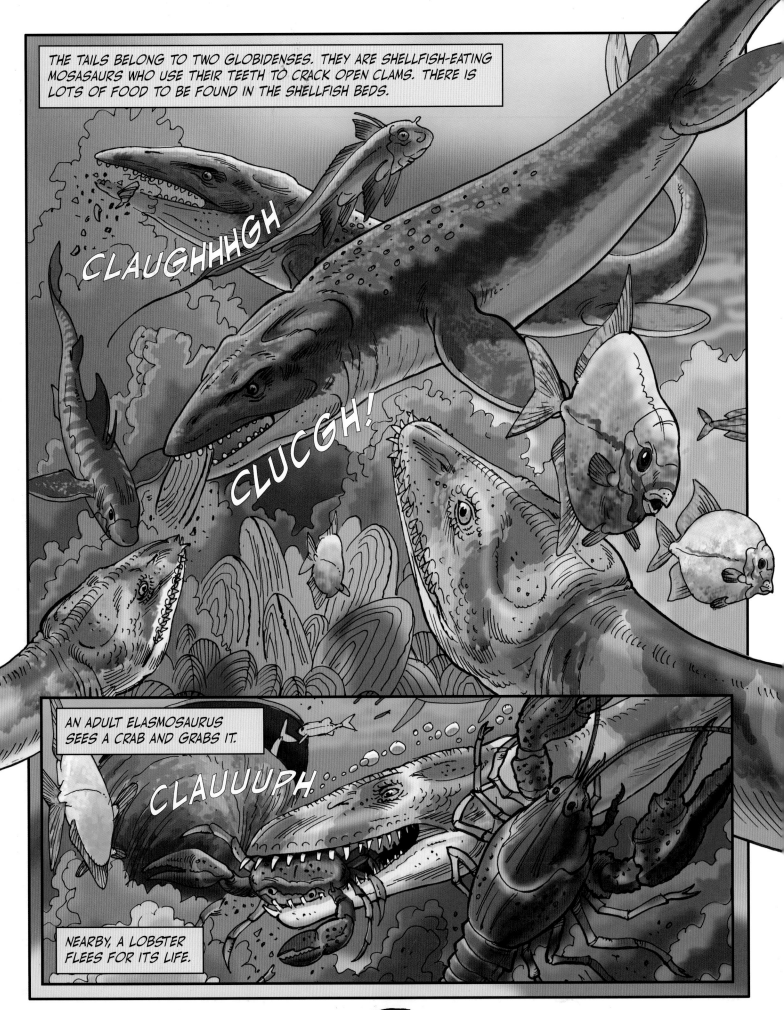

THE TAILS BELONG TO TWO GLOBIDENSES. THEY ARE SHELLFISH-EATING MOSASAURS WHO USE THEIR TEETH TO CRACK OPEN CLAMS. THERE IS LOTS OF FOOD TO BE FOUND IN THE SHELLFISH BEDS.

CLAUGHHHGH

CLUCGH!

AN ADULT ELASMOSAURUS SEES A CRAB AND GRABS IT.

CLAUUUPH

NEARBY, A LOBSTER FLEES FOR ITS LIFE.

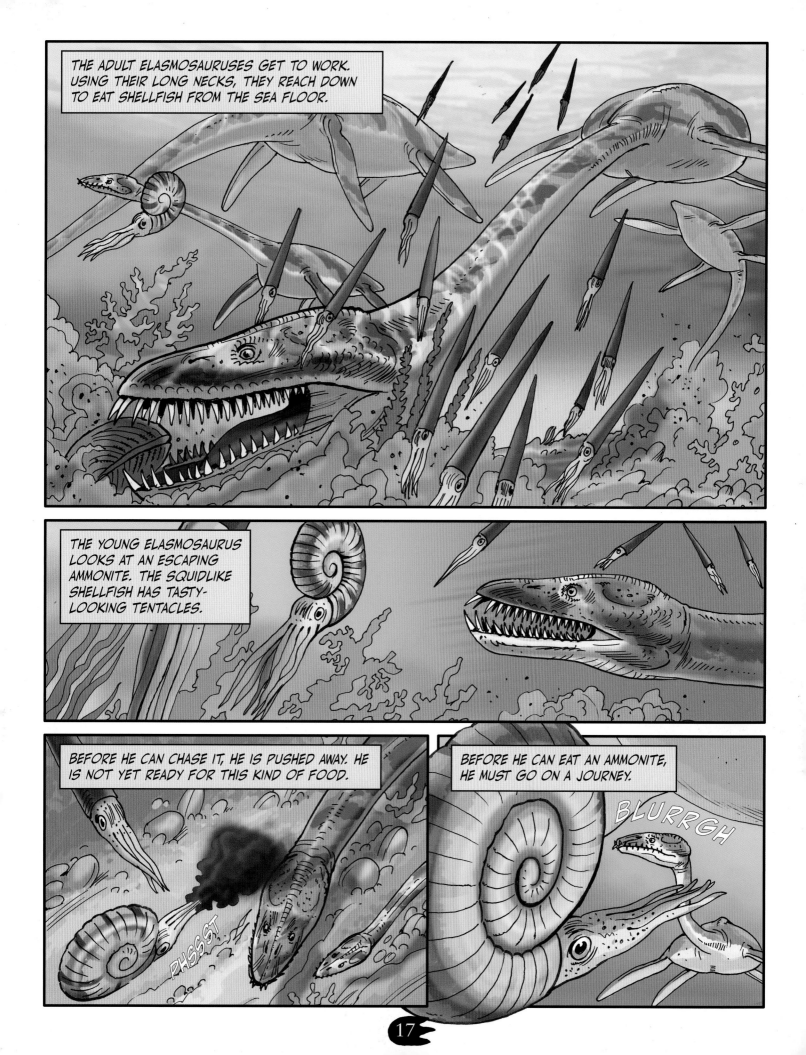

THE ADULT ELASMOSAURUSES GET TO WORK. USING THEIR LONG NECKS, THEY REACH DOWN TO EAT SHELLFISH FROM THE SEA FLOOR.

THE YOUNG ELASMOSAURUS LOOKS AT AN ESCAPING AMMONITE. THE SQUIDLIKE SHELLFISH HAS TASTY-LOOKING TENTACLES.

BEFORE HE CAN CHASE IT, HE IS PUSHED AWAY. HE IS NOT YET READY FOR THIS KIND OF FOOD.

PHSSST

BEFORE HE CAN EAT AN AMMONITE, HE MUST GO ON A JOURNEY.

BLURRGH

PART THREE... THE RIVER

THE ELASMOSAURUSES HAVE BEEN SWIMMING FOR MANY WEEKS. THEY HAVE TRAVELED HUNDREDS OF MILES TO COME TO A RIVER MOUTH.

THE ADULTS ARE LEADING THE WAY. THEY HAVE BEEN HERE MANY TIMES BEFORE.

THEY PASS A BEACH WHERE A TYRANNOSAURUS IS BUSY EATING A GIANT TURTLE.

PLOOOSH

THE TYRANNOSAURUS IGNORES THEM AS IT BITES INTO THE TURTLE'S SHELL.

KERRRUNCH

FARTHER UPRIVER AN ADULT ELASMOSAURUS LOOKS AT THE STONES THAT HAVE COLLECTED BEHIND A BOULDER.

HE SELECTS A HARD, BLACK PEBBLE...

KLOPH

...AND SWALLOWS IT.

GNURRGH

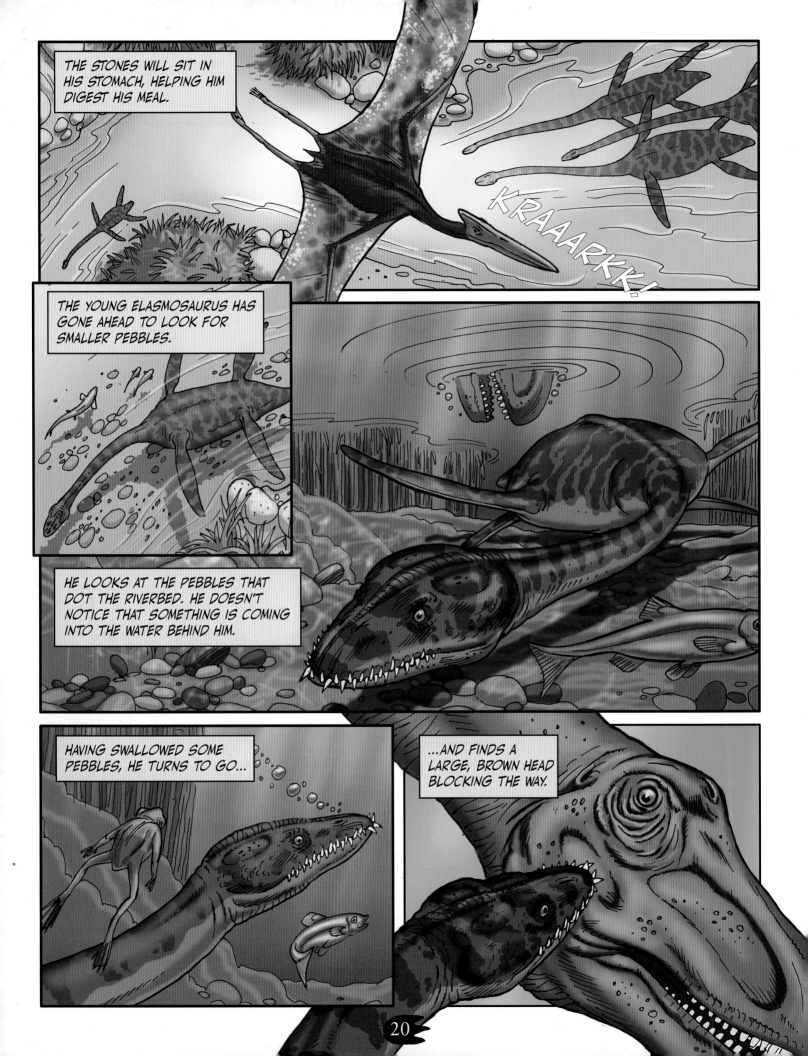

THE STONES WILL SIT IN HIS STOMACH, HELPING HIM DIGEST HIS MEAL.

KRAAARKK!

THE YOUNG ELASMOSAURUS HAS GONE AHEAD TO LOOK FOR SMALLER PEBBLES.

HE LOOKS AT THE PEBBLES THAT DOT THE RIVERBED. HE DOESN'T NOTICE THAT SOMETHING IS COMING INTO THE WATER BEHIND HIM.

HAVING SWALLOWED SOME PEBBLES, HE TURNS TO GO...

...AND FINDS A LARGE, BROWN HEAD BLOCKING THE WAY.

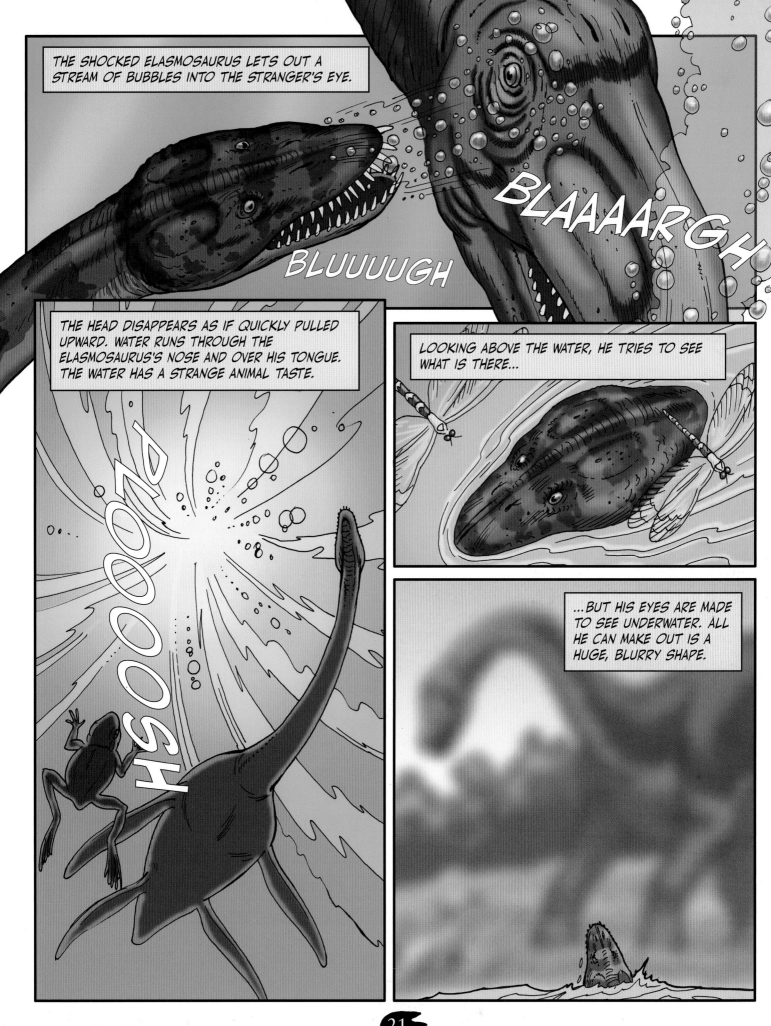

THE SHOCKED ELASMOSAURUS LETS OUT A STREAM OF BUBBLES INTO THE STRANGER'S EYE.

BLAAAARGH

BLUUUUGH

THE HEAD DISAPPEARS AS IF QUICKLY PULLED UPWARD. WATER RUNS THROUGH THE ELASMOSAURUS'S NOSE AND OVER HIS TONGUE. THE WATER HAS A STRANGE ANIMAL TASTE.

PLOOOOSH

LOOKING ABOVE THE WATER, HE TRIES TO SEE WHAT IS THERE...

...BUT HIS EYES ARE MADE TO SEE UNDERWATER. ALL HE CAN MAKE OUT IS A HUGE, BLURRY SHAPE.

THE BLURRY SHAPE IS AN ALAMOSAURUS, A GIANT PLANT-EATING DINOSAUR. IT IS STEPPING BACK OUT OF THE WATER.

BROUUARRRGH

GNAAARGH!

IT HAD ONLY COME TO EAT RIVER PLANTS AND IS NO DANGER TO THE ELASMOSAURUS.

HOWEVER, THE RIVERBANK IS CRUMBLING UNDER THE ALAMOSAURUS'S 33-TON (27,216 KG) WEIGHT.

ITS SMOOTH FRONT FEET SLIP IN THE MUD.

KLOMPH!

BROOUGHARR

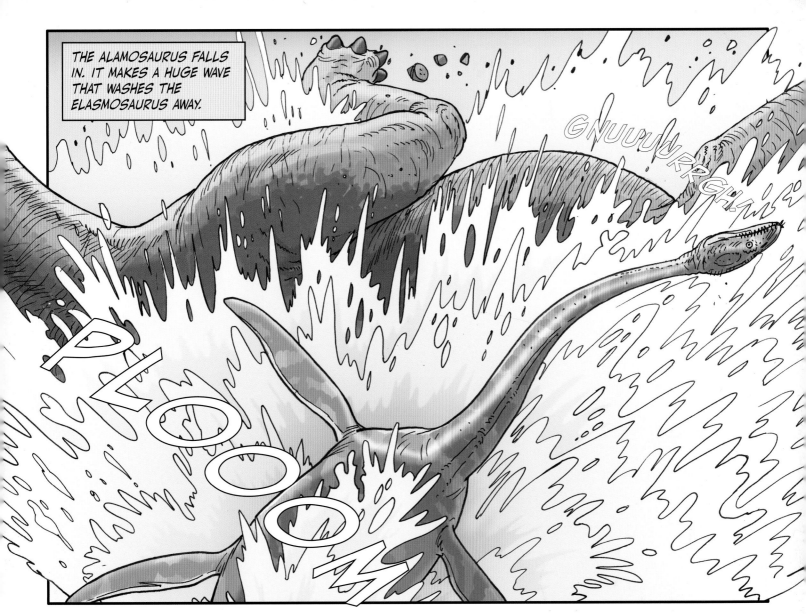

THE ALAMOSAURUS FALLS IN. IT MAKES A HUGE WAVE THAT WASHES THE ELASMOSAURUS AWAY.

GNUUUURRGH!

PLOOOOM!

HELPLESS IN THE POWERFUL FLOW, HE IS CARRIED DOWNSTREAM TOWARD THE SEA.

HE COMES TO REST AT THE RIVER MOUTH, BUT THERE IS NO SIGN OF HIS POD. THERE IS ONLY CLEAR, OPEN WATER...

...DANGEROUS WATER.

PART FOUR... TERROR FROM THE DEEP

AT THE RIVER MOUTH, THE ELASMOSAURUS SEES A FAMILIAR SHAPE SPEEDING BY.

IT IS A DOLICHORHYNCHOPS! SHE MIGHT LEAD HIM BACK TO HIS POD, OR, AT THE VERY LEAST, TO SOME FISH.

BLURRHWEEEEE!

THE HUNGRY ELASMOSAURUS FOLLOWS HER OUT TO SEA.

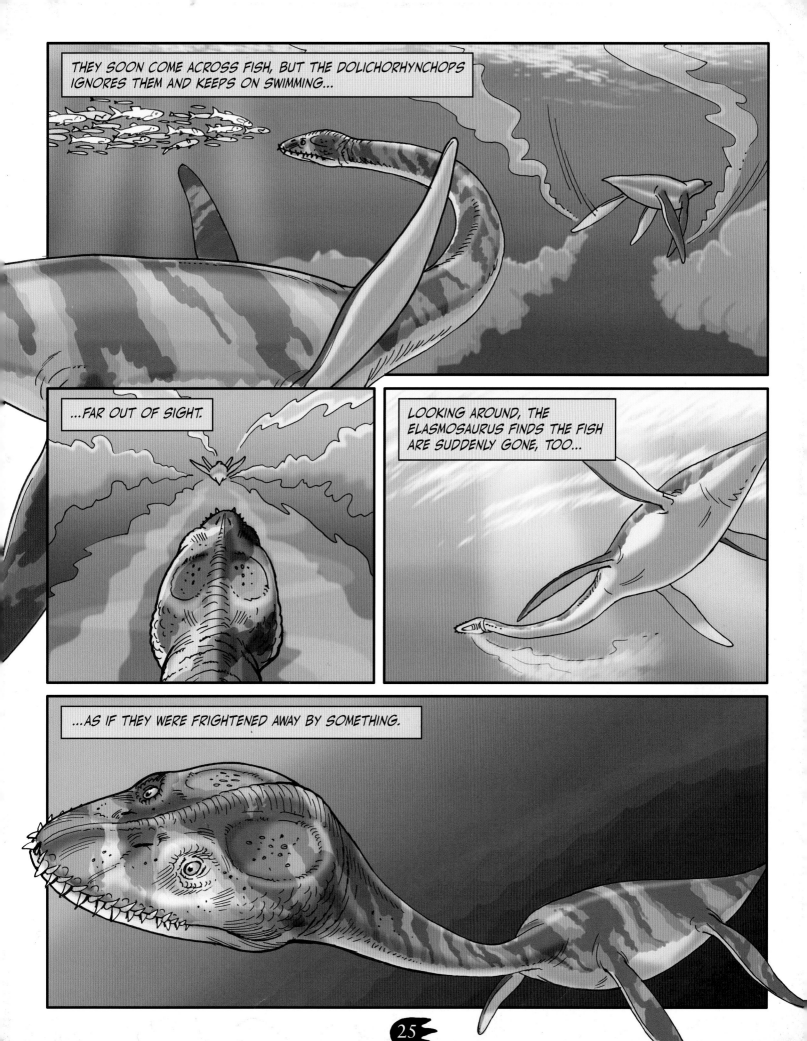

THEY SOON COME ACROSS FISH, BUT THE DOLICHORHYNCHOPS IGNORES THEM AND KEEPS ON SWIMMING...

...FAR OUT OF SIGHT.

LOOKING AROUND, THE ELASMOSAURUS FINDS THE FISH ARE SUDDENLY GONE, TOO...

...AS IF THEY WERE FRIGHTENED AWAY BY SOMETHING.

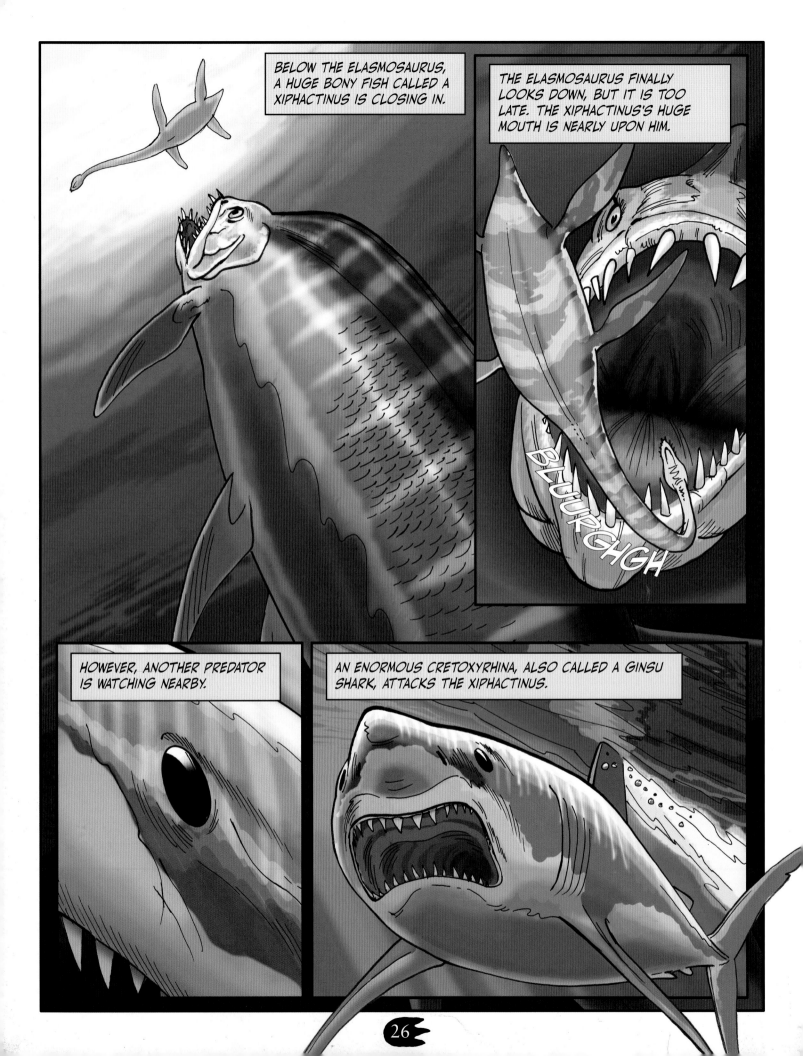

BELOW THE ELASMOSAURUS, A HUGE BONY FISH CALLED A XIPHACTINUS IS CLOSING IN.

THE ELASMOSAURUS FINALLY LOOKS DOWN, BUT IT IS TOO LATE. THE XIPHACTINUS'S HUGE MOUTH IS NEARLY UPON HIM.

BLUURGHGH

HOWEVER, ANOTHER PREDATOR IS WATCHING NEARBY.

AN ENORMOUS CRETOXYRHINA, ALSO CALLED A GINSU SHARK, ATTACKS THE XIPHACTINUS.

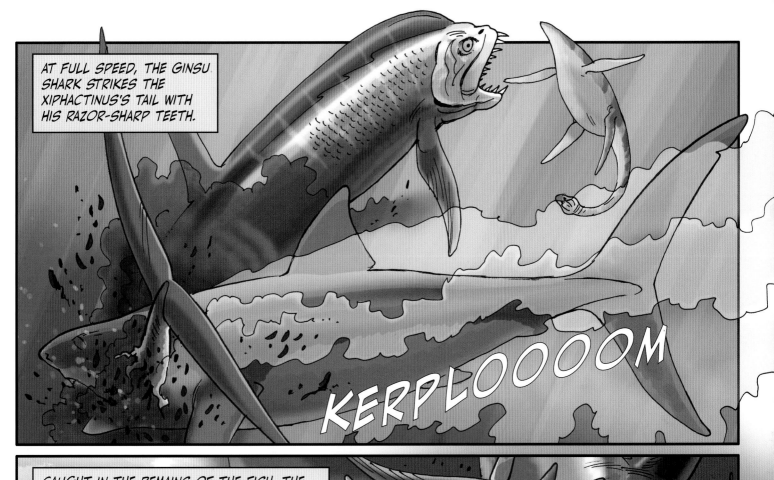

AT FULL SPEED, THE GINSU SHARK STRIKES THE XIPHACTINUS'S TAIL WITH HIS RAZOR-SHARP TEETH.

KERPLOOOOM

CAUGHT IN THE REMAINS OF THE FISH, THE ELASMOSAURUS IS HELPLESS AS THE SHARK SWIMS AROUND FOR ANOTHER ATTACK.

THE ELASMOSAURUS IS IN TERRIBLE DANGER.

THE SHARK'S JAWS ARE ABOUT TO CLAIM HIM...

...BUT, DEEP BELOW, SOMETHING IS WATCHING THE SHARK.

A GIANT MOSASAUR CALLED A TYLOSAURUS IS SWIMMING UP TOWARD THE SHARK.

GLAAAARRGH

THE TYLOSAURUS'S MOUTH CLAMPS SHUT, ITS TEETH BITING DEEP INTO THE SHARK.

CROMMPH

THE FORCE OF THE ATTACK DRIVES THEM BOTH UPWARD...

GRAARK

YARRK

PLOOOM!

...AND THEY BREAK THROUGH THE WATER'S SURFACE.

WHILE OTHER SEA PREDATORS MOVE IN, THE YOUNG ELASMOSAURUS ESCAPES.

BADOOOSH

AS HE SWIMS, HE SEES SOMETHING FAMILIAR IN THE DISTANCE.

IT IS HIS POD! THE ELASMOSAURUS RUSHES TO JOIN THEM.

LUCKILY FOR HIM, THERE ARE ALWAYS BIGGER FISH TO CATCH IN THE WESTERN INTERIOR SEAWAY.

FOSSIL EVIDENCE

WE CAN GUESS WHAT PREHISTORIC ANIMALS LOOKED LIKE BASED ON STUDYING THEIR FOSSIL REMAINS. FOSSILS FORM WHEN ANIMALS OR PLANTS THAT WERE BURIED TURN TO ROCK. THIS TAKES PLACE OVER MILLIONS OF YEARS.

Elasmosaurus's neck was as flexible as a giraffe's neck, and helped it catch its food. At the end of the Cretaceous period, Elasmosauruses faced strong competition for fish from mosasaurs. Elasmosauruses' long necks helped them find food on the ocean floor. This helped them survive longer than other big reptiles.

From looking at fossilized Elasmosaurus stomach contents, we know that they ate many different foods. Unusual items include parts of a pteranodon, which an Elasmosaurus probably found in the ocean. Elasmosauruses swallowed stones to help grind up the shells and bones in their meals, too.

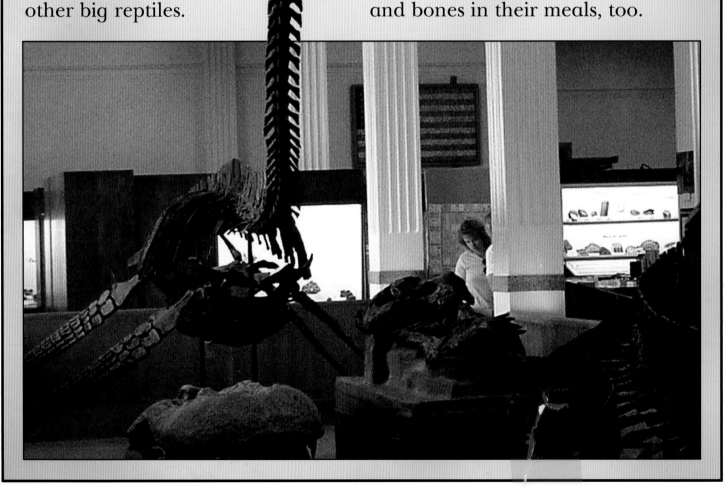

ANIMAL GALLERY

ALL THESE ANIMALS APPEAR IN THE STORY.

Hesperornis
"Western bird"
Length: 5 ft (1.5 m)
A large, flightless diving bird that preyed on fish.

Dolichorhynchops
"Long-nosed eye"
Length: 10 ft (3 m)
A short-necked relative of the Elasmosaurus.

Clidastes
"One who locks"
Length: 12 ft (3.5 m)
A sea reptile.

Globidens
"Globe teeth"
Length: 19 ft (6 m)
An unusual mosasaur that has rounded teeth for crushing shellfish.

Platecarpus
"Flat wrist"
Length: 20 ft (6 m)
A commonly found mosasaur that fed on squid, fish, and ammonites.

Cretoxyrhina
"Chalk sharp nose"
Length: 20 ft (6 m)
A shark the size of a great white shark.

Xiphactinus
"Sword ray"
Length: 20 ft (6 m)
A big, large-mouthed fish.

Tylosaurus
"Knob lizard"
Length: 42 ft (13 m)
A giant mosasaur that was king of the seas.

Alamosaurus
"Alamo lizard"
Length: 68 ft (21 m)
A giant plant-eating dinosaur.

GLOSSARY

Cretaceous period (krih-TAY-shus PIR-ee-ud) The period of time between 145 million and 65 million years ago.

darts (DAHRTS) Moves quickly toward something.

distance (DIS-tens) The space between two objects.

extinct (ek-STINKT) When the last member of a group of any living things has died out.

familiar (fuh-MIL-yer) Well known, like family members.

fossils (FAH-sulz) The remains of living things that have turned to rock.

pods (PODZ) Groups of sea animals such as dolphins, or elasmosaurs.

vanished (VA-nishd) Disappeared suddenly.

INDEX

Web Sites

Due to the changing nature of Internet links, the Rosen Publishing Group, Inc., has developed an online list of Web sites related to the subject of this book. This site is updated regularly. Please use this link to access the list:

www.powerkidslinks.com/gdino/elasmo/